Voice Lessons

Voice Lessons

Ramon L. Presson

Academy Park Press
Franklin TN

Published by Academy Park Press

an imprint of Williamson County Public Library

1314 Columbia Avenue

Franklin, Tennessee 37064

http://wcpltn.org

Printed in the United States of America

For My Mother, Frances Presson
With Gratitude and Love

*"I do not deny that there should be priests to remind us
that we will one day die.
I only say that it is necessary to have another kind of priest–the poet,
to remind us that we are not dead yet."*
— G.K. Chesteron

CONTENTS

Gratitudes

A Reader's Digest editor told an audience that a recent research study revealed three common elements present in the childhood of writers.

1) They loved books and enjoyed reading.

2) They were comfortable with and even sought solitude.

3) Their early writing efforts were encouraged and affirmed.

All three of those are true for me. I was an only child, very active and social, but also comfortable with the solitude and quiet of my room where I would read, write, draw, and listen to music. As a boy I enjoyed reading, especially the Hardy Boys mysteries. And I was the beneficiary of a mother who encouraged and affirmed my creative writing.

So the first person I wish to acknowledge and thank is my mother, **Frances Presson**, for playing that pivotal role early in the life of a young writer.

Others I wish to thank:

Maurice Thomas, an English professor and poet who came alongside during my first two years in college with valuable instruction and encouragement. I consider all of my poems to be his literary grandchildren.

Stellasue Lee, a twice Pulitzer-nominated poet and writing coach who moved right into my Tennessee subdivision and helped me first to recover and then to nurture the poetic voice I thought I had lost. Most of the poetry in this collection was written during or following being mentored by her.

Those Three Little Words

While there was a delay up ahead at the counter
I offered the lady in front of me a spare
copy of a 30% off coupon.
She looked at the coupon and
then back at me while her face imitated a sunrise.
"Oooh, I love you," she said.
I wish years ago I had known it was this easy.
Decades now lost, invested in offering
attention and affection, the currency of
quality time spent along with kind deeds,
thoughtful questions with interest in the answers,
romantic poems handwritten in calligraphy,
placing candles and arranging moonlight to
hit the window just so,
miles upon miles of garden walks,
handfuls of fresh cut flowers,
picnics with expensive Cabernet,
four seasons of conversation.
But now, only now, do I learn
that a bookstore coupon offering
a third off the highest priced item was
all that was needed.

Where Does the Time Go?

I tell ya, I just don't know where the time goes,
the postal clerk said to the customer
ahead of me, an older lump
with a plaid flannel beret and prickly ear hair.

I know where it goes, I said to her.
I know where time goes, I said
to the man with caterpillar eyebrows.

It slips out in a slow leak
like a tire that picks up a nail   *Psssssssssssssst*
If you listen real close you can hear it…
Psssssssssssssssssst

cause time whispers on its way out the door;
it doesn't bust out in a jail break killing the guards,
doesn't ransack the room while you're upstairs
sewing on a button.

Time is a runaway bride who packs a suitcase
while you're at work, leaves a note on the door
of an emptied closet, saying
"*Not happy. I don't feel important. Enjoy your career.*"

Weeks blow out the back of the truck like litter;
entire months are kidnapped by an obsession, years are stolen
like jewelry by a thief who'll make up special occasions
just to wear it.

Hours get spilled like a glass of beer or love,
minutes wasted like electricity
cause somebody left the light on.
Precious seconds go down the sink while brushing your teeth.

3

A lifetime peed and flushed when
rising in the middle of the night, the last morning
though you don't know it—your final birthday
in late October when the leaves in the Appalachians
are at their peak.

That's where the times goes, I said.

Oh, said the postal clerk.
Oh my, said the man.

Inscription Found in a Used Book of Raymond Carver's Poetry
at a Book Fair

Judith,
May these poems always lend you peace,
happiness, and make you smile.
Love, Marty

Marty, I don't know how to tell you this, but
the book is with me now. It's better this way. Forget her.
A woman who recycles a book of poetry is not worthy of your love.

Ray, this was not your fault. You did everything you could.

Hurricanes I Have Known

August 18, 1955, Hurricane Diane arrived ashore
near Wilmington, NC, and drove toward New England
on a killing spree.

I wonder how women named Diane felt about having
a murderous storm named after them. I'm guessing fewer
babies were named Diane in 1956.

In 1979 the first male hurricane was born. I don't know
how they tell the difference, but it only seems fair
that men share the blame.

I have a step-brother Andrew who suspiciously
shares the name of the 1992 hurricane that tried
to wipe us out when I lived in south Florida.

Now a sheriff's deputy in North Carolina,
Andrew is married to Elaine who
has a 2001 hurricane namesake,
apparently granted a second chance since
her 1974 event only achieved tropical storm status.

His mother Marie (2008, no landfall)
married my dad (Richard, 2010)
in 1987 (see Hurricane Emily, my step-sister).

I must mention my other step-sister
Rebecca (1968, off the coast of Mexico).
She battles MS and refuses to evacuate when
the storms come, and they come often.

My dad married Frances (2004, Category 2)
in 1957 (see Audrey, Category 4)
and in 1960 (Donna, holds Category 3 duration record)

I was born (Ramon, 1987, winds up to 135 mph).
The internet says, and I quote, "After peaking,
Ramon turned to the northwest and steadily weakened."
I find myself feeling a little defensive about that statement.

The report goes on to say that the heaviest rainfall
was confined to southern California, the post ending with,
"Ramon's impact elsewhere, if any, is unknown."

"Ramon's impact elsewhere, if any, is unknown."

How would you like to have that indictment
etched on *your* tombstone?

Please forgive me, I know hurricanes are violent;
and as selfish and uncaring as it may sound,
I would like to have a second chance.

Rain Song

When it rains all week like this,
when it drips, pours, soaks, and puddles,
mists, sprinkles, spews, and floods,
I'm afraid your moist lips might mildew
so bring them inside
and let them dry
on my neck and chest
while your wet clothes
hang by the fireplace.

Making a Child's Lunch

In Remembrance of Sandy Hook Elementary

While it is still dark
I take out the lunch makings for assembly—
things to slice, spread, and pack;
some things crunchy, some soft,
a mixture of items salty, plain, and sweet;

and I think of mothers and fathers
in a Connecticut town
who either cannot sleep
or who wish to do nothing else
but hide in a deep cave of sleep
where no nightmare can compare with waking,

parents who are making funeral arrangements
instead of repeatable lunches,
picking out small coffins
instead of pudding cups,
feeling a knife slice through the heart like soft bread,
the flat blade spreading unspeakable horror
and unthinkable grief to the four corners of a soul.

I think of twenty lovely children,
innocents trapped in a gallery of evil,
their blue vinyl lunch bags nestled in cubbies,
their names written underneath the lids
with permanent marker because
so much can be lost in the chaos of a day.

How to Read Poetry Right the First Time

My gosh, what are you doing? Do you
not know how to read a book of poetry?

It's not a newspaper, for God's sake;
you don't just read a poem like it's
an inked summary of a city council meeting or
the high school game that went into double-overtime.

You don't read a poem and just move to the next one
like you were collecting eggs or
putting Christmas catalogues
in mailboxes on a postal route.

Yes, there are kind and friendly poems
on adjoining pages but
that doesn't mean anything.
Gary Finke's memory on page 158 and
Stellasue Lee's grief on 159
have an ocean between them,

so don't think for a moment that
you can just walk out the back door
of one poem and stroll
through the front door of another
as if they were neighbors and they liked you.

The poem you were reading a moment ago
is a labyrinth, and you
are foolish if you think
you've made it out yet.

The Levine poem you've already forgotten
was a delicate package—a package
within a package inside a package and you

unwrapped it with a chainsaw.

That gentle-looking Mary Oliver poem in your hand
is a bomb that threatens to blow up
in your lap and in your brain, so to defuse it
you better know which color wire to cut.

Music in Black and White

On June 20th (my birthday), 1965 (I was five)
Ira Louvin, his fourth wife, Anne,
band member, Billy Barksdale and
his wife, Adelle, died instantly
in a collision with a drunk driver after
a show outside Kansas City.

The Louvin Brothers, Charlie and Ira,
were a highly successful country duo in the mid 50's.
They split up in '63 when Ira was playing
the bottle more than the mandolin.

My mother loved country music—
the old kind that reminded her of the Grand Ole Opry
on Saturday nights, her grumbling daddy
moving the large Philco radio this way and that
trying to get a decent signal.

Once tuned in, silence was ordered
and all the kids were told to go pee
before the Opry started because
"once Mamma's show starts you better
be dyin' if you move or make a sound."

My guess is that my mother didn't hear
about Ira Lovin's tragic death until June 21st
or maybe the next day,
so there was some other reason
she kept staring out the window
long after my father's Plymouth had left the driveway.

The Deer of Port Townsend

The deer are quite tame and plentiful in Port Townsend,
a delight to tourists from the mainland but
a bane to resident gardeners who lose their
freshman tomatoes and sophomore zucchini
to herds of soft, silent raiders.

A doe practically poses for me behind
the **For Rent** sign planted in the front yard
of a pale blue cottage,

as if you could rent a deer any more than
you could rent a cloud or
make a down payment on a sunset.

A few years back I did manage to
put a midnight rainstorm on layaway
for pick-up in late June when the beans
and melons crave natural water, knowing
a pair of fawns behind the folds of a draping fog
would enjoy freshly washed vegetables.

Romans 3:23–24

FOR ALL HAVE SINNED...

All have cut themselves while shaving
and are wearing tiny pieces
of toilet paper on their faces—
an unsuccessful veil
giving itself away
with its bright red dot like
a bullseye to target our gaze.

AND FALL SHORT OF THE GLORY OF GOD...

All have a run in their hose,
a hem held with tape,
a blemish beneath the make-up,
a wrinkle filled in,
a scar smoothed over.

BUT ALL ARE JUSTIFIED FREELY BY HIS GRACE...

But they are loved without their
masks and disguises,
repairs and enhancements,
without the fig leaves
sewn together with the faulty threads
of self-improvement.

The Kidney Stone

So this is a man's labor
and the best that he can hope for
from hours of sweat, pain,
water, blood,
contractions, and cramps—
the delivery of a tiny
crystallized thorn.

And in those tortured moments
he cannot fathom why any woman
would ever elect to have a second child
and Lord only knows why a third or fourth;

and with newfound insight and empathy
a man concludes that his own mother
is either an uncanonized saint
or was temporarily insane.

Down Tobacco Road

I'm from North Carolina, grew up
in Winston-Salem (no, they didn't
name the town after the cigarettes—
it was the other way around).

I attended RJ Reynolds High School,
the oldest high school in town. It
opened in 1923, still stands
as a monumental reminder that
tobacco built this town.

My grandparents on my mother's side
were tenant farmers—didn't own
the slat wood house, the fields,
or the tobacco barn.

I spent one young summer
stooped over row
after row of green stalks,
snapping the stems from the bottom rung
with a sweeping clockwise motion, my lower back aching
and my forehead dropping
sweat seeds into the soil.

I stacked the leaf fans into my arms,
walked to the end of the row and
would have just dumped them onto the wagon,
but my grandmother demanded that
the cash crop be treated with respect,

so I lined up the leaves and laid them down
like they were brand-new dress shirts, something
I never saw my grandfather wear
until the white one he wore in the coffin.

Living Large on a Sunday at Thompson Station Park

The late afternoon sun
borrows a cloud wisp for a prism near
a hot-air balloon so close I can
see the flame and hear the passengers in the basket
chatter about trying to make Leiper's Fork before sundown.

Low-lying spiders have spun glistening string art
from the tops of grass blades, and of the hundred or
so people in the park I'm the only one with the angle, the eye,
or both to see it.

Young lovers adrift on a blanket with sandwiches and Italian soda
sail past a boy lunging to catch a Frisbee and his father's approval.

And the cars in the gravel driveway across the way
are filling up with Methodists who missed it all
in exchange for a committee meeting.

What If…

What if every time we made love, you and I,
we conceived and delivered a full-term
newborn baby the very next day?

How poor and crazy do you suppose we would become
from housing infants to young adults
with a population, as of last night, exceeding
many small towns in Arkansas and all but
the largest cities in Wyoming?

Slip out of those day clothes and
come to bed, my love; bring the wine,
and prepare the nursery for triplets.

Why I Don't Believe in Karma

If it's true what they say——
that what goes around
comes around,
then karma is an old horse
slogging its way on a muddy oval track.

She is not a sprinter
running straight to the tape,
certainly no missile
heading for its target.

No, to wait on karma is
to straddle the hour hand of the clock,
waiting for 12
to become 12 again.

It is to make your bed on the planet Pluto
and wait out the 248 years it takes
for it to complete an orbit around the sun.

And when karma finally crosses
the cosmic finish line centuries later,
you've been dead so long
that not even your great-great grandchildren
are alive to know or care
that your justice and reward have arrived——
the bestowed blessing of the gods given to you
for telling that cashier at Kroger
that she gave you back too much change.

Note to Pablo Neruda

Pablo, I stopped by your poem today but
I couldn't get in.

I tried to enter at "*Assume a solemn voice and a*
protective cow's tone,
be decorated jointly
with Trujillo's envoy,
discreetly maintain
a garconciere..." but
it was locked tight as las puertas del infierno.

I tried it several times, rang the bell—no answer.
So I went around back to "... Araucaria, who are you?
Who am I? A subject!
Suffer! Subject! Run! Here I am!"

"Well, here I am!" I shouted.
The door was bolted and the shades
were drawn so I couldn't even peer in the windows.

None of the neighbors appeared to be home.
I guess I could have hung out there on the porch
till dark, broke a window, climbed in,
and taken a look around till the cops came,

but I was getting tired and
my Spanish isn't very good.

Love Is a Playground

My son is playing dodgeball on the playground
of his young heart, ducking and swerving
in order to be struck square by
the fickle affection of 7th grade girls.

Bethany has loved him twice now,
the sequel shorter than the original
which was but a brochure.

He doesn't understand the evolving and
revolving mind of the female, how to
jump on and jump off the merry-go- round
without being injured.

It reminds me of the trick we played on
one another in grammar school.
With our seesaw partner on the plank
lifted high in the thrilling air, we suddenly
dismounted which brought the mate
crashing to earth with a thud-clank.

I wish I could tell him girls will outgrow that,
but perhaps I should tell him that any time
his feet aren't touching the ground
he should always keep his knees bent.

Saturday Morning in Suburbia

Cardboard and poster board
yard sale signs at every intersection
and subdivision entrance
from here to the Maury County line,

these are the driveways where
we the middle class
set up our flea markets
and let total strangers
rummage through our belongings——

the discarded clothes, weary furniture,
and toys starving for batteries,
dusty paperbacks, framed prints,
dishes, and kitchen appliances,

clock radios, plaid throw pillows,
VHS movies, and the exercise equipment
we couldn't live without and
MasterCard said we didn't have to.

Now other suburbanites, like homeless people,
are going through our trash and asking
Does this work? and *How much
will you take for this cutlery set?*
when the homemade sticker with the price
is right there on the damn thing.

But everybody wants to talk you down,
as if you should give a further discount
for something that is already on
your entire life's clearance rack.

And you want to say "just take it", because

you know she doesn't want it that bad, but
she's addicted to mediocrity like everyone else,

like the lady there in the teal warm-up suit,
the one with board games in her arms
who said "I Do"

in the church to a guy she didn't really
have any use for, but he was a bargain and
she had a place for him next to the curio cabinet.

Autumn Is Lost

All these trees have timers on them, but
in the turbulence, the maples and oaks,
the birch and poplars, are leafy wind chimes,

so we don't hear the clock ticking
and we never imagine we'll be required
to rake up hopes once tender and green.

Rollercoasters in Real Life

steep vertical
slow climb
peak reached
dizzying height
brief pause
rapid plunge
blinding speed
upside down
right-side up
hairpin left
sharp right
final turn
sudden stop
let
me
out.

August 15th

On this date in 1954 Alfredo Stroessner
named himself president of Paraguay.
I don't know if it was only for that day but I
suspect that it was longer.

I've got a lot on my plate this upcoming week,
so I'm naming myself president of Paraguay
just for today. All government offices
in Paraguay are closed on Sundays,
so I don't suppose anyone will mind
and I don't think I can mess things up too badly.

I would like to have a parade through the capitol,
maybe encourage the national soccer team,
play a military joke on Uruguay, and
after a supper of asoda, chipa and boiled yucca,
get my portrait made for a postage stamp.

August 16th

On this date in 1962, Ringo Starr replaced Pete Best
as drummer of the Beatles,
a year before their first album.

Twist and Shout and *Love Me Do*
were on that record.
The concerts with layer upon layer
of screaming, crying girls soon followed.
I'm a guy and I was only three,
so I wasn't one of them.

I'm not really sure how it happened.
Maybe Pete thought the band wasn't
going anywhere. Maybe the rent was due
on the flat he was renting in Essex,
the one near the pub on Devonshire where
some of his old classmates and
some of the iron workers with bad teeth
kidded him about his sissy friends.
Perhaps the textile factory was hiring.

I think it worked out for the best because
Ringo Starr is a much cooler name.
I think you'd have to be in show business
with a name like that. No one would take
you seriously as a priest or an accountant.

But still I wonder about Pete.
We all know what it's like to disappear,
to watch a new employee or new lover
take our place. We've all come down
with some flu of regret that
made us sick to our heart.

Which one of us has not been forced
to watch replays of our misplayed fold
and the smile of the opportunist who
swept the hand and cashed our chips.

I hope Pete had a good life, I really do,
that love followed him where
fame begged off, and that drumming
his fingers on a satisfying glass of dark ale
was music and riches enough, knowing
that celebrity is just obscurity biding its time.

August 20th

It was 1804 on this date that Charles Floyd died,
the only member of the Lewis and Clark
expedition to perish. Clark wrote in his journal,

"Floyd died with a great deal of composure.
Before his death he said to me, '*I am going away,
so I want you to write me a letter.*'
We buried him on the top of the bluff,
above a small river to which we gave his name."

Turning 50 in June did not disturb me.
Instead it was today that
age arrested me where I stood
with the thought of death, knowing
that good health and safety can be temporary as
a full sun and a cloudless sky.

It was the hinting which deafened me,
that death is the great Interruption,
the grand Cancellation, that one's expedition may
be in mid-route when it is halted.

It is not the journey of books and prose
that I fear being clipped,
but the poetry. I have hundreds of poems
floating in a pond known as a blog,
and nowhere else.

They are neither bound together, nor
even printed alone in isolation.
They're saved in clouds, with
volumes more inside me.

But this truth haunts me: that so many

of us die with our collection incomplete—
an anthology of pieces never printed,
with still more verse yet composed.

And thus we die
atop a bluff above a small river that
won't remember our name;
and with much poetry lodged within us,
we plead for a scribe to write a letter.

August 23rd

I don't really care what happened
on this date in 1674 or 1733,
or what made news on August 23rd
in any year of the 1800's,
like the 1866 Prague Treaty,
Britain's 1939 taking of Hong Kong,
or even Mexico declaring independence in '21.

I don't care about Beeldenstorm reaching
Amsterdam in 1556 enough to even mention it.
The crowning of King Philip VI of France in 1328
doesn't interest me in the least.

When Count Gyula Karolyi became premier
of Hungary on this date in 1931, I'm sure it
garnered attention in some circles but
it didn't even register on my radar.

It's Monday, August 23, 2010,
and that's what matters,
but the day is three-quarters over
and I haven't done anything that
would make headlines in an anthill.

I'm tired. I have bruised ribs I hope
aren't cracked, and having to breathe
made last night a fitful sleep.

Chicago Cubs outfielder Sammy Sosa once
fractured a couple ribs during a violent sneeze.
No, it wasn't on this date and, even
if it was, I would not care.

August 27th

(for Nicole and Jay)

Hemmed in by two world wars, on this date in 1928
the Kellogg-Briand Pact was signed by the USA,
France, Britain, Germany, Italy, Japan,
and over 50 other nations renouncing aggressive war
as "an instrument of national policy."

Since it's our anniversary, I was wondering
if we could call off the war,
outlaw all skirmishes and battles,
quell any riots that might spring up
among disgruntled workers in this relationship.

I'd like to go to the harbor tonight, just the two of us,
not as tugboats with children, but as a sleek quiet
schooner that takes the wind instead of fighting it,

and maybe we'll turn back the sails and
lie in them as sheets of a king-sized bed,
and waste the generous space of it
by meeting in the middle.

Without Poetry

Dear reader, what would you do
if I stopped writing poetry, if I
ceased bringing cut flowers in from the garden
and placing them in vases by the breakfast nook?

What if I milked the moon almost dry
so there was never more than a crescent
in the midnight sky?

What if I stopped noticing deer on the hillside,
forgot to call your attention to the way the fragrance
of honeysuckle rides the breeze like a ghost ship,
if I kept the wine to myself and no longer spread
the picnic blanket beneath the large oak at the park?

There's always a remote chance I could stop
hearing the songs of whippoorwills or the voice
of God in a young child whose bounce threatens
to unsaddle the pale blue ribbon from her ponytail.

But it's OK because you'll be too preoccupied
to notice that I've become too busy
for quaint descriptions and metaphors, that
perhaps I've grown weary of taking inventory
in earth's store, or am exhausted from taking up
Adam's mantle and naming all the animals
(both inside and surrounding me).

You and I, we'll go our separate ways and you'll find
a newspaper to read, an investment magazine,
or a romance novel, and I'll work the Jumble,
write serious books, and tell the writers group that
poetry is nice but it doesn't pay the bills.

Then again, perhaps one day so far flung from now
that I don't even recognize you,
you'll stop me on the street, on the corner,
just as I'm preparing to cross, you
with the tired coat and trembling hand,
asking me if I can spare a poem.

Room for Cream

In polite robotics the barista asked me
"Do you need room for cream?"

Yes, and room for sugar and a dull spoon,
and room to breathe, room to heal,
room to make mistakes, space enough between liquid and lid
to be completely confused, to ask questions
which lower a rusty bucket
into the depths of this muddy brew.

I need room for a sequestered jury. I could use
a few acres near the river
for a monastery, a bar, or both.

I need room for history, an allotment for a library
of telling volumes, an eleventh-floor beach-front suite
with a balcony and a bedroom larger than my insecurities
and my measuring up
to a vaulted ceiling of comparisons.

So yes, if you're pouring all of me into that paper cup,
please leave room for cream.

Postcards to America

This is my obligatory poem of European travel sites
sprinkled throughout the piece
like *les chaises sur la café trottoir.*

My reading of other poets tells me
this is a required element
much like the salchow
in a figure skating competition or
including flairs and scissors on the pommel horse.

Should I begin by telling you about the faded pattern
of the curtains draping my breezy window overlooking
the Piazza Santa Croce?

Or should I tell you about Spain, about
the near-perfect seaside villa of Mazarron and
the school girl who giggled at my froth mustache
as I sipped my ristretto from the tiny porcelain
cup, the delicate handle no bigger
than the ear of a field mouse.

How tepid would your life seem
with its day at the lake and
burger cookout if I spoke of France,
if I went into even the very
minimum of details about making love
in the moon-drenched dunes of Villefranche, drunk,
though with class, on a bottle of Chateau Simard
which was purchased, intending only to toast
our broker and congratulate our good fortune
in finding such a quality camembert in the market.

Perhaps I should hurry and
tell you about Cologne and Frankfurt

before you lose interest, or pretend you are still
reading this while I paint you a picture
of a mundane moment in Lanarkshire.

Wait, don't go; give me your address and
I'll send you a postcard from Luxembourg with
a cube of commentary I know you'll love.

And when you get my letter
handwritten in the pub
with a pen carved out of mahogany
by an artisan I ran over
with my moped outside Brussels,
you won't be surprised to learn that there
are no trailer parks in Venice.

I Could Live Without Romance

Oh sure, I could live without romance.
For centuries people lived without electricity,
running water, or
even walls to hold up a roof
to keep out the gods' wrath.

Large cities—actually,
there are entire nations that wring out a living
from their wet rags without
benefit of clean water, education,
or professional health care.

I guess I could live without passion
if most people can live without poetry,
even if I can't. Me, I can't go a day without
sitting with Donald Hall at a New England window
or without trying to coax Emily Dickinson
to come with me to a county fair.

Some people survive with
only one kidney or just
one good eye, or
with no feeling in their legs,
or between them.

More people than not somehow
have survived without ever tasting
Moravian sugar cake, or
a fresh peach so sweet
it doesn't need sugar.

Imagine not hearing so much
as a single note of Mozart or
never making love in candlelight

while guided by Vivaldi
through tastes and touches
unknown to angels.

People have lived very productive lives
without ever having seen
Colorado in autumn when
entire slopes of aspens
spin their green leaves into gold.

I have it on good authority that
there are people right here in Franklin who
have never tasted a really good Chardonnay,
people whose thirst for beauty can be satisfied
by trips to Gatlinburg.

So yes,
I could probably live without romance.
A life without the kind of passion
that makes me spin around in circles
with my eyes closed until I fall
dizzy and spent
against her neck.

I could try living without all that, if
you call that living.

Ode to Raspberries, Well…Not Exactly

I'm not very fond of raspberries and
I promise it has nothing to do with
the silent "**p**" that is a useless and wasted
letter there in the word, as far as I'm concerned.

Oh sure, it's in the team photo, but
it's a bench rider;
it never gets in the game.

Nobody's asking me, but I recommend trading it
to a word like "pupil" or
"palpable" as an understudy or a back-up
in case one of the starting "**p**"s goes down.

Perhaps offer the "**p**" to a foreign word and
throw in the "**s**" in exchange for
a premium "**z**" because raspberry
is begging for a "**z**."

But I know how these things go.
The government will concern itself with
health care reform and immigration, and the
general public is preoccupied with
the Red Sox losing streak.

Meanwhile, an innocent letter
is doing a life sentence
inside a word prison, while I seek to
bring attention to the injustice of it all
with my complete boycott of the fruit.

Sleeping Through a Magic Show

Seated on the front row
on the far left beyond the sight
of the U.S. Poet Laureate on stage,
reading his poetry

a man, slumped in his soft seat,
resting his jaw in his cupped hand,
his eyes closed.

Maybe he's a light sleeper
and the storm last night kept him awake.
Perhaps he had too much pasta and wine
at Trattoria's for dinner.

He could be closing his eyes
to sweep the room of distractions,
the way one closes the eyes while making love
or listening to Beethoven.

I suspect that he is simply numb to beauty,
and was being lulled
by the gentle and steady fountain of words,
a magic unknown to him, a language
more foreign to him than Latin.

Maybe he was coerced to attend,
dragged here like a cinderblock pulled by a rope.

What poverty to live in a mind decorated only with prose,
landscaped with nothing but sentences of vital information.

In a moment he will be startled out of
the opening stanzas of his dream by our applause
and wonder what wonder he just missed.

Voice Lessons

Megan, I understand that you are taking voice lessons
on Fridays after school. Thirty minutes one-on- one
with a retired professor from Juilliard
in her Tudor home where nothing is out of place except
a worn husband and too many cats.

Megan, I think you should know that tamed and trained adults
with holes in their swimsuit pockets
where the wonders fell out, will tell you that
your sandcastle voice is built too close to the surf.
They'll offer you a relocation package and help rebuild your skill set,
even guide you in digging a moat that love cannot cross.

Having lost my own voice off the tee somewhere
in the tall grass when I was about your age,
can I whisper to you some subversive advice?

Run, Megan! Run, sweetheart!
Run for the door, run over
your teacher, past the used-up man,
through those stupid cats, out the front door
with its Mozart doorbell, carefully
but quickly down the calculated steps
and when you get to the swept and pressure-washed sidewalk,
don't look back.

Your mom will be there in the driveway,
trying to stay warm with the engine turned off,
faintly singing a tune you wouldn't know,
her eyes moist, her nose pressed against her window like a child
peering into an aquarium, wondering what it would be like
to be a fish.

Megan, this is your getaway car so tell Mom to step on it!

Because you just robbed the bank where they were holding
all the play money, magic, and silliness of childhood.

She'll hesitate, your mother will, but tell her to drive
and to keep driving. Then tell her to head to the park—
the one with the bridge and picnic table near the stream,
the one with the monkey bars and swing sets lit up
in primary colors. She'll start to get it, Megan.

She has more to pass on to you than imported olive skin
and silky brown eyes.
She understands more than you think,
which is why she often wears sunglasses
on these overcast and overspent days.
But don't probe her on that.

Instead may I suggest that you invite her to pick out a CD
and a favorite song for the ride?
The two of you should sing along quite loudly.

By the way, don't let anyone convince you that
singing too forcefully will cause you to lose your voice.
On the contrary—that's how you'll find it.

So sing loud, Missy. Belt it out, and if you miss some words
and massacre a few notes, all the better.
Don't sing precisely, but passionately
as if your life depended on it

because it does.

Enough Already

Enough about snow drifts in the foothills
and icicles hanging from
the porch roof. Enough about sleet against windows,
candle reflections, and all things lunar.

Enough about fireplaces and slippery curves, about
snowballs, sleds, and warm lips. Enough already
about red wine and ski gloves,
and the sound of children playing outside our window.

Get to the good part,
the part where the sun
comes over the hill a champion,
bearing melt and thaw like weapons,
kisses the frozen garden, and
sends the children back to school.

Florida Room

I wish I was writing this today from my Florida room,
not the airy solar-warmed addition on the back
of the house, walled by glass, fused with natural light,
ceiling fan moving slow enough to count the blades,

hanging baskets of ferns taking the soft
sun of morning, one African violet that thinks
it has found paradise next to
a bowl of pears on an end table,

strong coffee in a china cup sweetened
with brown sugar cubes from
a tiny bowl with matching lid, a yellow
pencil reclining on a white bed of paper,
a finished poem resting by my arm
like a satisfied lover.

No, I mean an actual Florida room—a room in
Florida, preferably south Florida,
specifically a Palm Beach room,
to catch the morning sun and
a room in Naples in the late afternoon
when the sun lies down on the ocean
and dims the day.

Actually, almost any room in Florida will do,
just a warm room with a window, or
maybe one overlooking a stand of palms
and a tree of Honeybells where I plucked
a perfect orange for breakfast.

I Must Be Going

I sit close enough over the fire
to feel the flame tongues lunge at me
like a dog in the lap
trying to lick my face.

I've been told I don't have enough
respect for fire
or for lightning.

Maybe not since the time I had it sizzle
all around me on a Colorado mountain;
so perhaps now I feel invincible or
maybe I just think nature is a poor shot,
a near-sighted sniper who misses his target
99.9% of the time but has managed to
keep his job and the villainous reputation;

or maybe I just think it would be too comical
of a way to die——walking on a golf
course cursing a 4-iron and suddenly
I'm aluminum foil in a microwave oven.

I don't like to think about how I'll go,
or when—if I'll go sudden like lightning
or if I'll just fade out slowly
like a fire unattended.

In Praise of Dependable Counseling Furniture

You think I'm just an ordinary couch,
don't you? Just another sofa
in this (or any other)
wrinkled second-hand store
with one dim-lit employee
who doesn't know squat
about fabrics or wood grains.

OK, so you sat one family for a lifetime
of T.V. shows and rented movies,
faces aimed straight ahead on parallel lines
that rarely intersected, voices muted
by a universal remote, hearts unplugged,
knees that didn't touch.

Me? I've listened to a thousand stories
from a single-file parade of the soul starved
who waited their turn, held their place
in line with their teeth, gripping their pull-off number
in this deli queue for the disordered
like it was a winning lottery ticket.

I've kept the secrets of villains and
victims, have filed between my cushions
the case notes of betrayals and addictions, longings
and lostings, body sins and head wounds,
and the heart explosions which I muffled
and absorbed with no telling stain.

Live to Fight Another Day

I bent straight the hard curves on Kedron Road
to race a tornado home, screamed at
by sirens to go faster, faster,
faster, you idiot, if you expect
to make it in time to rope
your children like calves
into the cellar, deep into the dark of it,

far from the plywood door that
has only a latch on the outside,
a flimsy one that will break like a cigarette
so the door can be splintered and
ripped off its hinges.

No alternative but to stand outside the thin door,
weaponless, show no fear
cause a twister can smell fear.
It'll stalk a weak animal,
chase it down from behind,
catch it, roll it,
pin it, shred it.

But not if I rage against the beast,
charge it, dare it,
mock it, bait it
into a bar fight.

I skid the car in the aggregate driveway,
rush inside, where my wife
asks me if I would like a brownie.

Magic Show

As adults we know that magicians are actually illusionists.
Interestingly, we do not resent their deceiving us,
but think of them as entertainers.

But when it comes to love, we hunger to believe
that there is indeed a deep magic,
a true magic that is not sleight of hand.

And, with our own heart up on the stage
as an audience volunteer,
we are comforted to see God
wearing short sleeves.

Leaving Well Enough Alone

The open fire is small and contained,
inviting a close chair, a pipe,
and a glass of wine,

the flames casual and hypnotic,
an orange glow in the timber cellar,
throbbing, making the wood
crackle and hiss, a faint whistle
from inside the grain.

I'm grateful for this slight breeze north
that leans the smoke back, and I don't know
how long I've been staring into
my tiny arson.

With an iron tool I poke the embers,
maneuver the kindling, and
adjust the planks though they are ripe
right where they are.

Why is it so hard for us to
just let good things be?

October in Tennessee

A hot air balloon is coming in
over the tree line, which
is the right thing to do on a Sunday afternoon
when the oak shadows are edging
across the field.

I'll sit here with my bought coffee, and
pretend it's better than it is,
till the tip of that tallest shadow
reaches the fence by the stables.

It seems so long ago that I secured
the patent on my life, and I can only
guess how many more autumns I have
to complete the project.

The shadows have wrapped their fingers
around the pickets, so I pull the plastic lid off
and pour out the remains of the day—
a good day, the sun and the craft aloft
setting on opposite ends of the earth.

Poetry Tax

I put our tax returns in the mail today,
enclosing checks in amounts that if
paid in cash would have made the envelope
nine months pregnant with twins.

It got me to thinking, what if other things were
taxed in the manner of income—this slicing off
a wedge of wealth as though it were a hoop of cheese.

Property tax might mean removing bricks from
the south side of the house this year,
perhaps the roof next year if the appraisal goes up,
along with two Douglas firs and a bed of day lilies.
I'd need to give the cardinals and finches a heads-up that
I can't guarantee the bird feeder will survive the cut.

What if children were a tax liability instead of a tax credit?
"Yes, we graduated our oldest boy last fall, the youngest
is playing soccer, and the IRS took our middle child
back in April. We do miss her so."

What if they taxed poetry?
Reduced my word count,
nickel and dimed me on adverbs, took a clever or
critical line when a throwaway would do.

Maybe they'd tell me to send in the second stanza
of *Love Is a Playground* plus three haiku.

Then again, what if I've prolifically written myself
into a higher tax bracket?
Will it cost me *Voice Lessons*, *Down Tobacco Road*,
and *Room for Cream*?

Maybe they don't check that closely. Maybe I could
send them someone else's poems, like
Locklin's *The Iceberg Theory* or
maybe *Things My Father Said* by Stellasue Lee.

If audited, perhaps I'll bribe the agent
with Simic and Burkowski, maybe
slip him a Keats.

Midlife Chrysalis

I'm looking at this cover of *The New Yorker*,
an artist's rendering of a pigtailed youngster
gazing out the back window of a pale sedan
laden with vacation gear on the roof rack.

In the upper right-hand corner
in Bookman font is
July 26, 2010,
and it strikes me that the year itself
looks like a futuristic, space-age number
quoted in a black and white sci-fi flick or
a Saturday morning cartoon when

I sat alone in the floor of our
brick rancher on Rushland Drive
with a bowl of Cocoa Krispies
just a few feet away from the Magnavox
which stood completely still
for most of my childhood on four spindly legs.

It never moved from its centered spot on the paneled
west wall of our living room, under the clock
that has never been replaced, as if the hands
of an old time piece can hold everything else
still around it, or at least slow down and
direct the traffic around it.
But it can't.

The wild frontier date in the upper right-hand corner
tells me I'm fifty years old, and that seems impossible.
I'm still being formed, still taking shape, with
too many unfinished parts
to be born prematurely into midlife.

But maybe it takes becoming a half-century
to realize you are becoming a whole person,
that no thing, no person,
no place or experience,
no achievement
need be added to make you complete.

And while you continue to grow,
you discover that everything you need to flower
is already present in your stem.

On the Back Deck at Dusk

Storm approaching, wind is picking up,
the trees bent and swaying, the leaves
showing their pale underbellies.

Fresh ground, fresh-brewed coffee
with a single sugar cookie from the trio
I bought at the bakery. The tinkling
of the spoon against the china
sounds like tiny wind chimes.

This is the first night of summer
I have seen fireflies.

They're striving to hold their lanterns
steady in the wind, tiny
runway lights by the garden,
showing my worries where to land.

Last Poem

After writing and sending off a new poem
you always fear maybe that was the last one,
like sending your daughter off to college and suddenly realizing
that child
was your youngest.

You pen the last line, edit a few words,
change a line break or two and light the fuse to
launch it. And for a moment
you panic because you still have a forest of matches
but only a cellophane wrapper empty of fireworks.

You give the poem a fashionable title and
then wonder if that was your last clean shirt.

Maybe in the morning you'll head to the barn and
find you used the last cord of wood,
gathered the last reluctant egg.

Plus every insecure new poem knows he's being
compared to prior lovers and suspects he'll be found lacking,
so in a move that either postpones judgment or
confesses inadequacy the poem says to the reader,
"I was wondering if we could just cuddle tonight."

Decision Making

Jane: "Lizzie, are you alright?"
Elizabeth: "How does one know?"
—*Pride and Prejudice*

A breeze is blowing here atop the hill, but
I must watch the direction
the branches bend, and
the angle that the leaves fall
to discern the wind's course

because my skin
is such a poor compass

and the erratic flight
of butterflies is a contradiction
even on a still day.

Rain Barrel

Why does everyone have to make
so much noise at 6 in the morning?

With their bare feet on the hardwoods, doors
and drawers opening and closing, clothes hangers
scraping on the rod, spoons clanking in cereal bowls,
shampoo bottles falling in the shower, hairdryer
on low, books being stacked, papers shuffled,
backpacks zippered, school bus striving up the hill,
a bird singing under the awning.

Will everyone please get to
the places where they need to be!
I need everyone to be quiet so I
can lie here in my dark room
and listen to the rain fall.

It's not enough to know it's raining,
or even see it. I need to hear it——a steady rain,
not aggressive but firm,
not a flooder but a cleanser,
to wash out the dust and leaf pollen
in the air, the bird droppings off the car,

rinse grief off the sidewalk, disappointments
and lingering hurts off the steps,
get at resentments stored
deep in the wood on the back deck.

Let the downpour loosen lofty goals
and ambitions from the roof,
collect in the gutter, then
pass through the downspout into the ground.

Let the pooling run down the street against
the curbs toward the storm drains,
taking with it regrets and humiliations,
defensive pride that rises up
when I feel foolish or underestimated.

And by all means let the streams converge and
boil in their meeting, and let them swirl all around
the pitch of earth they would trap in the center, but
be assured they will find hope to be
a most stubborn and sturdy island.

Rethinking Romance

What if romance is overrated,
you know, like Memphis barbecue, the Beatles,
and French women?

What if you're really just paying for the name?
What if passion is just effective branding with an Apple logo,
slick marketing like Starbucks that has
everybody paying four dollars for frizzed coffee
when it's half the price at Waffle House with free refills?

Maybe the benefits of romance are over-stated.
What if romance is being hawked
by snake-oil salesmen and it can't
really cure whatever ails you?

What if romance is twirled by spin doctors and is just hype
like the newest diet book or acai berry colon cleanser?
What if romance is nothing more
than a campaign promise?

How many of you out there, raise your hands, did passion
promise the world and didn't even deliver New Hampshire?
Do you really want to pin all your hopes on a fairy's tail?

And how do we know that romance won't go out of business?
If Kodak and Pontiac bit the dust, what chance
does the big **R** have if sex doesn't make budget?

What if we're holding out like virgins
for scented candles, wine, soft jazz, and shaved legs
and we're all gonna die before the honeymoon?

What if we're all binging on sappy post-it notes,
karma sutra, meaningful conversation, and

cuddling during movies, and the truth is
this shower isn't big enough for two?

Maybe Victoria's Secret is
that Hanes is just as good when running errands
or when cooking for a man who doesn't notice that
when you reach for a glass in the cupboard
a black knit top has a way
of rising and revealing
the creamy curve of hips.

God as Punctuation

Maybe God is the apostrophe in contractions
like Can't, Wouldn't, Won't
warning against every action
with a Shouldn't and a Don't.

Or maybe He is the apostrophe
of the kind that notes possession
to remind us what and who is God's,
halting this it's-all-mine obsession.

Maybe God is the hyphen
that bridges things separated.
Or maybe God is the dash,
life between my birth—my death yet dated.

Ramon L. Presson
1960 — ?

Then again, maybe God is parentheses
and everything's contained in Him,
bookends holding upright life itself,
banks securing the river within.

If God is a comma,
then there's always something after Him
like a conjunction, a noun, or adverb,
but then He'd never show up at the end.

OK, so maybe God is a period.
The dot that says we're done.
But there's no end to infinity
so He keeps marching on.

So maybe God is the ellipsis…

the symbol of continuation,
tiny stars at the end of thought
to follow with imagination...

Maybe God is an exclamation point!
Maybe He speaks and stamps his foot,
fearing that if He were too subtle
we wouldn't know where He stood.

If God is quotation marks,
is it because He likes to hear Himself talk
and be quoted verbatim and inerrantly
lest He say nothing at all?

Myself, I see God as a question mark,
the most profound riddle and mystery.
Because just when I've got God tamed and figured out
He slips up from behind and surprises me.

Seeing Clearly in the Dark

I am up this morning before the sun, before
the dew, before the morning glories' yawn,
before the enterprising early bird,

before the worm,
before the dawn clears its throat,
before the paper boy's coffee, even before
a train whistle so far in the distance it could
be yesterday or tomorrow,

before a cardinal leads the nest in an invocation, and
several delicious minutes before
a barking collie becomes the starter's pistol
that begins the day.

Ode to a Park Bench

The plaque on the park bench where I'm sitting says

**In Memory of
Malcolm Moss Gibbs**

Mr. Gibbs, if you knew the deep thoughts
I've had here on your bench,
the questions sent and returned
as unanswered mail, the prayers interrupted,
the anguish served raw, and the dozen or so poems
docked and launched from this port,
maybe you'd finally know you died
for a good cause.

Please forgive me for not introducing myself before now.

The Book Signing

Oh favorite famous author,
will you autograph my book, please!

Would you sign it on the title page,
on the spine, and inside sleeve.

Would you sign the preface and epilogue,
and the covers front and the back.

Please sign the table of contents,
not the foreword——someone else wrote that.

Please sign the acknowledgements and endorsements,
and the ISBN number, don't forget.

Oh my! You want MY autograph first??
Oh...on the lower right side of my check.

The Problem with Living Next Door to the Perfect Husband

She sees me, my neighbor does,
through her parted curtains
making my way up the sidewalk
toward the front door and my porch

with a modest bouquet of fresh-cut
yellow daisies from the market,
and she hates me for it,

almost as much as she despises
her tepid husband, an emotionless tap
who on occasion accidentally leaks a kindness.

She hates surprises, these
tokens I bring home with petals and baby's breath
or with a light cream cheese frosting,
knowing they will be arranged in a crystal vase
or served with steaming peach mango tea

while Jim brings home beer breath and short fuses,
stains in the armpits of his drab white shirts,
presents her with boredom and sarcasm, and
the expectation of cold sex on demand.

While I unloose the ribbon and trim the fibrous stems
to make them better straws, she would like to
slice off my fingers, lining them up on the acrylic board
where she is cutting up chicken for a meal
they will eat in well-rehearsed silence,
exchanging the salt and pepper shakers
and sections of the newspaper.

To Miss Alice Brewer At South Fork Elementary

You probably won't remember me but
in 2nd grade you gave me a D in handwriting.
It's never bothered me nor
made me resentful in the least

which is why I've spent years
tracking you down to your
current address in a nursing home
to let you know that I harbor no ill will

as evidenced by this handwritten note
penned exquisitely in calligraphy
in a special patented font
that I designed for Hallmark.

Please note how the poles
on the lowercase letters *b*, *d*, and *h*
are the exact same height as any capital letters,
as if all were barely touching a ceiling
made perfectly even by a carpenter with a level.

Observe how the tails of the *p*, *q*, and *j*
descend and trail into a flourish
like the train of a royal wedding dress.

You're probably thinking back to those sheets of paper
we practiced writing our letters on——that off-white paper
with the solid and dotted blue lines there to guide us.

Looking back, I see them now as bars
on a bird cage or prison cell
that confined my freedom
and held my creativity hostage.

You'll notice I have written this note on blank paper,
the letters flowing and the lines floating in air,
yet straight and uniformed as a troop of inky soldiers.

From the fine lettering on the envelope,
you probably mistook my parcel
for a graduation announcement
or a wedding invitation

But this is neither;
as I was unable to locate you in 1978
or again in 1987
but God knows I tried.

Write-In Votes

I'm calling for a do-over election with more room
for write-ins of things trustworthy and pure.

I elect the dawn's deer grazing at the edge of a Franklin pasture.
I elect the inhaling and exhaling of the surf at low tide.
I elect the sounds of children playing
in a limited-edition Tennessee snow.
I elect the steaming cup of coffee before the sun comes up
and morning hits its stride.

I elect the birds at dusk crowding the lobbies
of favored trees at check-in.
I elect the warm flood in the chest
that accompanies the first sip of good wine.
I elect the smell of fresh cut lumber and its running mate,
new leather.
I elect the *Welcome to North Carolina* highway sign
that reminds me where I was born and which land raised me.

I elect the dogwood tree in my backyard
that blooms on cue at Easter.
I elect the daring sparrow at an outdoor café that snatches
a muffin crumb that fell from my plate.
I elect the honeysuckle along a backroad when the fragrance
hitches a ride on the breeze.

I elect the mornings in Evergreen, Colorado
where Mount Everest rose in the distance
and tipped his snowcap to greet me.
I elect the vows that a new book and reader make to each other
before getting undressed.
I elect that which cannot written in on a ballot,
that which will guide us forward, ever forward,
regardless of who lives in some white house.

As a Member of Poets Anonymous

I really tried NOT
to write any poetry yesterday but...
I couldn't help myself.
There's so many triggers.

Just a phrase, I said to the bartender,
at most a haiku.
Do not pour me a sonnet even if I beg.
Just a taste of sound will do me, and I'm certain as sunrise
I won't pull a Milton
and end up face down in an epic.

But when the poetry flows,
regardless of who buys,
I forget all responsibilities to my day job
and my night family, and I'm ready to
put the complete works of heaven and hell on my tab.

I don't resist and hold up well—not when
Michelangelo himself sculpts the clouds
over the north ridge like he did today,
not when two unrelated objects connect the dots
and discover they are cousins,
not when an old love song beats me up in a back alley.

I left the bar early tonight,
passed a bookstore on my way home,
and I don't remember buying the 6-pack.
I thought perhaps I could just *read* the poetry.
Just hang out,
watch and listen,
maybe smell the imagination on Ted Kooser's breath
without craving it. Ha!

For me reading Billy Collins is the step right before
ordering a Tom Collins, and then the next thing I know
I'm so drunk I think I understand T.S. Eliot.

Back home, before I could call my sponsor,
I was tossing back shots of the color lavender,
the sound of the word eucalyptus,
and the silky feel of her breath draped around my neck.

I drowned my sorrows and joy by binging
on a January landscape where everything green and worthy
had been blown off,
frozen off,
killed off, or
put to sleep.

I twisted the cap off something better left unsaid
and took a long draw of the fire
so the burn could slide down like lava.

Regret is a great sipping whiskey,
but it goes straight to the head on an empty stomach
and straight to the toilet after that.

I poured doubles of unrequited love
on the rocks, a steady stream of verse
that eroded and smoothed the jagged edges,
slicked the stone tops
so that I fell trying to cross.

I know, I know; I should have stopped writing
and poured out the rest,
but I probably would have gotten my
tongue stuck in the drain.

I need help; I know that.
I've got unopened poems hidden under my car seat,
a few publishable ones ......shhhhhhhhhhhhh!
....stashed behind the canned goods in the pantry.
Some half-written pieces jammed in my desk drawer and
a file full of cold drafts wedged in between my passions
and my common sense.

I'll have one helluva hangover in the morning, surrounded
by wadded-up empties on the floor.
I'll probably go to confession,
re-dedicate myself to prose and journalism, to something
that sells and tells people what to thinkfeeldobelievesaywant.

I'll sober up and write my column for the newspaper and tackle
the Chapter 5 re-writes of an overdue manuscript.
Cause poetry is cotton candy—pink sugar air fluff on a stick.
You can't live on something which has no nutrients and
just evaporates in your mouth like that.

Poetry is peppermint schnapps, candy cane liqueur
so sneaky that, before you know it, your liver is as shot as your
punctuation and line
breaks.

So I'll really try NOT
to write any poetry tomorrow
but...

I don't know if can help myself.

There's so many triggers.

www.ingramcontent.com/pod-product-compliance
Lightning Source LLC
Chambersburg PA
CBHW031931090426
42811CB00002B/149